SO-ANP-588

sent betwe

disag

they talked to ea

village in a once u

country words

chaos

disord

mona

igno

frustr

chaos differ

in confusion

kept

lived in contusion
in a once upon a time
not tell
babies
together
worst
monotonous
terrible
different
they
who
chaos
howled
their wives
ran under the big tree in
worst thing about
reached the middle

For my dear friend Franny —— C.A.

Text copyright © 2022 by Caroline Adderson
Illustrations copyright © 2022 by Roman Muradov

Tundra Books, an imprint of Tundra Book Group,
a division of Penguin Random House of Canada Limited

All rights reserved. The use of any part of this publication reproduced, transmitted
in any form or by any means, electronic, mechanical, photocopying, recording,
or otherwise, or stored in a retrieval system, without the prior written consent of the
publisher —— or, in case of photocopying or other reprographic copying,
a licence from the Canadian Copyright Licensing Agency —— is an infringement
of the copyright law.

Library and Archives Canada Cataloguing in Publication

Title: Babble! and how punctuation saved it / Caroline Adderson ;
illustrated by Roman Muradov.
Names: Adderson, Caroline, 1963— author. | Muradov, Roman, illustrator.
Identifiers: Canadiana (print) 20200211455 | Canadiana (ebook) 20200211463 |
ISBN 9780735265837 (hardcover) | ISBN 9780735265844 (EPUB)
Classification: LCC PS8551.D3267 B33 2022 | DDC jC813/.54——dc23

Published simultaneously in the United States of America by Tundra Books of Northern
New York, an imprint of Tundra Book Group,
a division of Penguin Random House of Canada Limited

Library of Congress Control Number: 2020936742

Edited by Tara Walker with assistance from Margot Blankier
Designed by John Martz
The artwork in this book was created digitally.
The text was set in Baskerville and Times New Roman.

Printed in China

www.penguinrandomhouse.ca

1   2   3   4   5   26   25   24   23   22

Penguin
Random House
tundra   TUNDRA BOOKS

Babble!

AND HOW
PUNCTUATION
SAVED IT

WORDS BY
Caroline Adderson

PICTURES BY
Roman Muradov

tundra

I

in a village called Babble in a once upon a time
country there were people who lived in confusion
when they talked to each other they could not
tell the difference between what they were saying
and what they were thinking all the words just
ran together and parents were irritated with their
children and the children were irritated right back
at their parents and with each other the babies kept
crying and the dogs ran under the big tree in the
yard and howled but maybe the worst thing about

this terrible situation was that everything these people said they said in the same flat monotonous voice until one day someone came walking into the village she was small enough to be a child maybe she was a child she wore clothes that were older than she was and around her neck hung a cloth bag on a string when she reached the middle of the village where the monotonous babble was the most concentrated she put both hands over her ears and said stop

but no one heard her

so she went and sat on the edge of the fountain and took the bag from around her neck she opened it and shook into the palm of her hand something too tiny for anyone else to see now and then she poked at the thing with her finger and smiled

eventually a bawling baby came crawling along the stranger leaned down to show him what was in her hand all at once the baby stopped the irritable mother of the baby noticed him at the feet of the stranger and rushed over to pick him up she clutched him hard and glared at the stranger as though she had intended harm though the mother was frightened and angry she was unable to raise her voice instead she said in that frustrating dull monotone you have something in your hand

in truth she did not know if she really said it or if she only thought it but she must have spoken for the stranger showed her what it was to the mother it looked like a freckle or a speck of dirt it looked like this

●

The mother wanted to ask what it was for but could not.

It is to help people understand each other the stranger said.

2

The stranger let the mother hold the . on the tip of her finger. The mother brought it very close to her eyes.

I can hardly see it she told the stranger. Or perhaps she only thought it. It was impossible to tell.

The stranger spoke again. You see it better when you use it because it makes whatever comes before it stop. And she showed her.

Like this. Look.

The mother was amazed. But she was even more amazed when the stranger asked her to lift the tiny thing to her ear.

What do you hear the stranger asked.

Nothing she answered. Or thought she did.

Exactly the stranger said.

Oh it is so lovely and quiet the mother said.

And now you can think about what you just heard. Now you can make sense of it.

With her baby on one hip the mother turned and started to walk away with the quiet . As she passed the other villagers in the street babbling monotonously they suddenly stopped. In silence they began to follow her. She walked all through the village and up and down every street and by the time she circled back to the fountain where the stranger was sitting the whole village was with her and no one was saying a thing. Or maybe they were just not thinking anything.

This is the person who brought this to us the mother said or thought. Carefully she held out the . for the stranger to take back.

3

The people of the village were grateful for they could not remember a time when they were not babbling meaninglessly. But they were still frustrated. They could not tell the difference between speaking and thinking. Neither could they express the feelings that they felt. Not even their frustration. They had so many questions for the stranger. Questions no one was able to ask. Or think. So they all just stood and stared at her.

They watched as she took the bag from around

her neck again and dropped the ● back in it. She
tipped something else carefully into her hand.

It looked like this

The stranger asked why are you so irritable all the time?

The villagers looked at each other. Though they certainly felt irritable and frustrated they had never before asked themselves why. They could not. Some of them looked at their feet in embarrassment and others scratched places that did not actually itch. Finally a boy stepped forward and answered the stranger. Or perhaps he only thought he did.

I am irritable because I do not understand.

Will this help? the stranger asked.

The boy took the ?. Then he passed it to his father.

Why are you always babbling at me? he asked. Or thought.

Am I? the father said.

Yes.

Do you not know that I love you?

No the boy said.

Do you know now?

Yes the boy said.

The father and the son hugged.

4

Once all the villagers had a chance to hold the **?** they were bursting with questions. Who is talking? Who said that? Was it me? Am I speaking or am I thinking? How can I tell? Who is this stranger? Where did she come from? Why? What else does she have in her little bag?

I came to help you the stranger said.

Help us how? they asked. At least they thought they did.

To help you punctuate.

What is punctuate? they asked.

The stranger held up her bag.

How can that help us?

It helps you understand.

How can that be true? someone asked. I have so many questions. Before I had none. Yet I still cannot tell if I am asking them or thinking them.

If I am only thinking them who will answer me?

I have questions too someone else said. Who can tell me why my dog stands under the big tree in the yard and howls?

Me too. Why can I not spit watermelon seeds as far as my brother can?

Who asked that?

No one. You thought it.

Then why did you answer?

I thought I heard it.

Who are all these people asking questions?

Why am I so confused all the time?

Here the stranger said. Try these. And she shook something new out of her bag and threw them into the air.

"Do these help?" she asked.

"They help a lot" said the boy who could not spit watermelon seeds as far as his brother could.

5

Now the villagers looked around in wonderment. When they opened their mouths the " and the " made the words come out.

"Why do my pajamas have pockets?" asked a curious girl. "What would I carry while I am asleep?"

An old woman stepped forward. She felt the " working on her lips and tongue and the " pushing the words out. "My granddaughter asked that. I heard her with my own ears."

The villagers could not believe it. The words leaving their mouths were different from the ones that stayed inside their heads. They could finally distinguish thinking from speaking.

But that was only part of their astonishment. Now they heard how the **?** made their monotone voices rise like birds lifting into the air.

"Do flowers fall in love?"

"Will my baby toes ever grow up?"

"Can anybody guess that I am wearing my underwear inside out?"

The villagers did not care if anyone answered their questions or not. They just stood around enjoying the sound of their own voices.

"Do you live in the house across from mine?"

"What is your name? Why do I not know it?"

"Is that your garden on the corner? How do you get your cabbages to grow so large?"

"How many children do we have?"

"Would you like to come for tea?"

While the grown ups were talking the children did what children have always done even once upon a time. They made up a game.

"What did you dream about last night?"

"Was it a bear?"

"Do you often dream about bears?"

"Did you think it was true?"

"Is this a dream?"

"Is that a bear coming up behind you now?"

6

All the people in that once upon a time village were so busy questioning each other that they did not notice a child running away.

The child was full of fearful thoughts. Is the bear chasing me? Should I look back?

Something did come up behind her then. She nearly jumped out of her skin. But it was only her dog. He had followed her as dogs have always done even once upon a time.

"Is there a bear?" she asked the dog who of course could not answer. She felt safer now with the dog beside her. Together they walked down the path to the river.

"Thank you for coming with me" the girl said.

The dog wagged its tail affectionately for no one had ever spoken to him in anything but that maddening incoherent babble that made him go stand under the big tree in the yard and howl.

As they reached the river the girl remembered all the things she had once wondered about the river but had not been able to ask. Where did it start? Where did it end? Why was it flowing so fast? What was the hurry? Was something chasing it?

She decided to ask the river. "Are you running from a bear?"

But her voice was too quiet under the roar of the current. The girl edged down the slippery bank closer to the water.

"Help" she said in her quiet flat voice. "Help me I am going to drown."

No one heard her.

7

"Why is that dog howling like that?" the children asked themselves.

"What is the matter with him?"

The dog was annoying them by nipping and trying to interrupt their game.

At last a boy noticed something. "Where is my sister?" he asked.

By then the stranger had called out to the dog. Out of her little bag she took a stick and a ball.

They looked like this

!

Sticks and balls are the favorite things of dogs now and once upon a time. The stranger threw them to the dog who caught the stick and the ball together and ran off.

A moment later a faint cry sounded. "Help! Help!" But it was not loud enough.

"Use two!!" the stranger shouted and threw another ! to the dog. The dog raced away again.

"Help!!"

"Three then!!!" She threw another.

"HELP!!!"

Finally the drowning child got the attention of the villagers who all rushed to the riverbank where the dog stood barking his head off. The father of the girl reached out his hand. "Take it" he said.

But she could not hear him over the rushing water. She flailed her arms helplessly and one of the ! flew right out of her hand.

Someone caught it. "Use this!" He passed it to the father.

"Grab it!" the father shouted to the girl.

The girl did and was saved.

8

"What is it? What is it?" everyone asked after the girl had been pulled to safety. "What is that thing that saved her?"

Before the stranger could answer them the shivering girl began to shout. "I am alive! I am alive! I am alive!"

They all fell back in amazement. It was not just how loudly she spoke but the joyful expression in her voice.

"Where has the ! gone?" everyone asked. "I want to try it."

"There were three a minute ago."

"The dog ran away with one."

"No. I took them back" the stranger told them. "I have to show you how to use them. The ! is special. You must save it for emergencies. Otherwise it will lose the special power it has."

"Is it really only for emergencies?" asked a disappointed villager.

"Emergencies and when you find yourself in a noisy place. And when you really need to express yourself. When your heart will burst otherwise."

"We love you!" cried the father and mother of the girl who had nearly drowned. "We love you! We love you! We love you!"

"Like that" the stranger said.

9

How much better life was in that once upon a time village! They could stop talking whenever they wanted and just sit and savor the peaceful silence. They knew they were speaking when they spoke and that they were thinking when they thought. They could ask and answer questions. Their voices rose and fell. They could shout as well as whisper. And the stranger had been there only a few hours!

The people were so happy that they decided

to throw a big feast. All afternoon they rushed around getting ready. They set up tables around the fountain. They ran home to cook. The children climbed the trees and hung streamers.

"Look at me!"

"Watch out!"

"Aaaaaahh!"

Meanwhile the stranger sat on the side of the fountain watching the comings and goings with a smile.

As the afternoon wore on the villagers asked the stranger if she would take the place of honor at the head table that night and share their meal with them.

She told them "I am sorry but I cannot."

They were surprised. Then they were worried. "Have we done something to offend you?" they asked even though the stranger was smiling. She did not seem at all offended.

"I cannot join you because I do not eat people. I do not eat people or cats."

It was the villagers who were offended now. "Eat people? Eat cats? We would never do that!"

"We are not cannibals!"

"We are not catibals either!"

"But I heard you say that you were serving Grandpa."

Everyone stared at her.

"It was you." The stranger pointed to a woman. "Soon we will eat Grandpa. Is that not what you said?"

The woman stared in horror for she had indeed said this to her old grandfather so frail and helpless.

The stranger pointed to a man in a barbecue apron. "You said you loved cooking your family and your cat. Did I hear you wrong?"

The man in the barbecue apron grew red in the face. His wife and children gaped. The fur rose on the back of his cat.

All at once everyone was shouting.

"This is disgusting!"

"Barbaric!"

"I am not going to the feast either!"

"I am going to throw up!"

All the cats ran up the trees while the dogs stood under them and howled.

"Please! Please! That was not what I meant!" begged the two accused.

"Stop!" cried the stranger. "Stop right now!"

Everyone fell silent. She took off the cloth bag and tipped something tiny into her hand. It looked like this

,

She gave it to the woman who had told her old grandfather that they were going to eat him. She tipped another out of the bag and gave it to the man in the barbecue apron. "Try them," she said.

The woman turned to her grandfather. "Soon we will eat, Grandpa."

The old man smiled, relieved it would soon be dinner and that he would not be on the menu.

The man in the barbecue apron announced to everyone, "I love cooking, my family, and my cat, but not necessarily in that order."

"Oh, Daddy!" cried his two daughters. "You scared us!"

He hugged his girls and his wife. His cat purred and rubbed against his legs.

The stranger passed the , out to everyone. She said, "These are really useful. Now you can be perfectly clear about what you want to say. You can also do more than two things now, one after another or at the same time."

"Yes, I see," someone said. "I can agree, nod, and understand."

"I can steal a bun, climb a tree to eat it, and shout things down to annoy my sister," a boy said.

"You can annoy more than one person too," the stranger told him.

"Yes! I can steal a bun and, laughing, climb a tree to eat it, then shout things down to annoy my sister, father, mother, aunt, uncle, and all my cousins!"

His sister said, "And I can shout back at my smelly, bun stealing, repulsive little brother to get down from that tree right now!"

When they had finished laughing, the stranger showed them more useful things. If they put the , high instead of low, like this ', then they would not have to brush the beard of their grandpa. They could brush Grandpa's beard.

They would not have to kiss the cheeks of the baby. They could kiss the baby's cheeks.

That wasn't all the ' could do. Sometimes the villagers's tongues tripped inside their mouths. But not anymore. Now two words could become one with the help of the '.

"Aren't you hungry?"

"Can't we eat now?"

"Don't you want to sit beside me?"

It seemed to every single person who lived in the once upon a time village that they had a lot to celebrate.

"Once upon a time it seemed as though we were living in darkness. We didn't listen to each other. We didn't understand one another. But now we understand. We communicate. We love!"

compassion

unity sense

conversation

empathy

air

sensitivity

understand

consideration

understanding

compassion

comprehend

love   unity

warmth

sensitivity and

kindness   love

consider

communication

warmth

compassion

sensitive
time
communicate.
sion   comma
unity   consi
ndess
love   love   unic
ding   con
mpathy   kindness   emp
mth   comp
npassion
we understand
understanding
communicate

Afterword:
More Punctuation!

There are more punctuation marks that you can use to express exactly what you want to say. Also, they look quite fancy. You should try them!

PARENTHESES separate explanations within a sentence.

> Punctuation (the marks used in writing that clarify meaning) is important for communication.

A **DASH** can interrupt a sentence.

> Without punctuation, it's hard to underst —— We can't really communi ——

The **ELLIPSIS** shows that parts of a sentence have been left out or that thoughts or speech have trailed off.

With punctuation, the meaning of a sentence becomes clear and we can avoid confusion, misunderstandings, hurt feelings **. . .** and all other forms of miscommunication. Well, usually **. . .**

A **SEMICOLON** connects two related ideas in a sentence, each of which could stand alone.

Some people express themselves clearly **;** others just babble.

The **COLON** can be used to make lists.

Here are all the punctuation marks you read about in this book **:** period, question mark, quotation mark, exclamation point, comma, apostrophe, parentheses, dash, ellipsis, semicolon, and colon.